LOVE IN ACTION

To Doris Hoesman
For Faithful
attendance

Solomon Lutheran
Sunday School

Sept. 12, 1976

LOVE IN ACTION

E. JANE MALL

> "My children! Our love should not be just words and talk; it must be true love, which shows itself in action."
>
> 1 John 3:18
> *(Good News for Modern Man)*

Concordia Publishing House
St. Louis   **London**

Concordia Publishing House, St. Louis, Missouri
Concordia Publishing House Ltd., London, E. C. 1
Copyright © 1971 Concordia Publishing House
Library of Congress Catalog Card No. 79-162530
ISBN 0-570-03127-3

MANUFACTURED IN THE UNITED STATES OF AMERICA

Dedicated to Ray and Ellen, who are constantly striving to be little Christs in the world—and they achieve it an amazing number of times.

I was hungry,
and you formed a humanities club
and discussed my hunger.
Thank you.

I was imprisoned,
and you crept off quietly
to your chapel in the cellar
and prayed for my release.

I was naked,
and in your mind
you debated the morality
of my appearance.

I was sick,
and you knelt
and thanked God
for your health.

I was homeless,
and you preached to me
of the spiritual shelter
of the love of God.

I was lonely,
and you left me alone
to pray for me.

You seem so holy,
so close to God.
But I'm still very hungry
and lonely
and cold.

(Anonymous)

We don't have family devotions anymore. When the children were young, family devotions were an important part of each day. When our evening meal was finished, we pushed back our plates, and Carlton got the Bible and whatever devotional book we were using (mostly we used *Little Visits with God*). Carlton read the Scripture passages, and one of the older children would read the devotional material. Then we would all join in a discussion.

After Carlton died, we kept on with our daily family devotions. They were a necessary part of our growth, and we all learned much during those years. Then we grew up.

As time passed and the children grew, I began to see that there was a sameness about our discussions and that more and more often I found it necessary to say, "You aren't listening!" or, "Did any of you even hear one word I just read?" The eagerness with which the children had put the Bible in front of me,

or begged to be allowed to read the Scripture passage, had vanished. It had been a long time since any of them had said, "Don't forget our 'votions, Mom!"

I spent some foolish, wasted hours mumbling about the generation gap, youth of today, etc. and etc. And then I saw that this had nothing to do with a generation gap or the youth of today. The children were bored, and I didn't blame them. We were still operating in a kindergarten situation when we had long ago graduated to a much higher grade in our understanding of faith. I would certainly know that something was wrong if my child grew physically, year after year, but was still kept in kindergarten in school. Why hadn't I seen that they were advancing and maturing in their faith as well?

There is devotional literature written for the teen-ager, the mature person, etc., and much of it is excellent, but it's mostly private. I encourage the children to read devotional material and their Bibles every day. But what we needed as a family was something whereby we could exercise our faith, learn more about God and His will, together, the way we'd done with our daily "'votions." The pace of our world today is such that young people aren't attracted much to a more or less forced feeding of Scripture and comments on the way of God in our lives. Maybe we wish this weren't so, but we have to deal with what is, not with the way we want it to be. Baseball practice, homework, dates, all contribute to the scattering of the family, and most of the time the members of the family simply aren't all together at the same time, usually not even for one uninterrupted hour a day.

Family devotions provided a wonderful togetherness, a daily opportunity to talk together as a family unit about our faith, what was expected of us as Christians, and a cementing together as we joined hands around the table and prayed. It's still almost obligatory for the Christian family with young children.

I wanted to recapture all of this through another medium. Because of the faster pace of our lives, and the children's rejection of family devotions, it looked very difficult, if not hopeless. But I was determined. This was too precious a thing to let slip away from us. "Somehow," I said, "God will show me a way."

And, of course, He did. I don't recall exactly how it dawned on me, but one day there it was. I knew the children had heard from infancy what our Lord has done for us, what He expects of His followers, what real, deep-in-the-heart faith is. They had been taught that it meant much more than warming up a pew on Sunday mornings; more than dropping some money in the collection plate. Much, much more than being able to say, "I went to church this morning."

They had known these things for a long time, and now they wanted to be about their Father's business in the world. They wanted to start exercising their faith that was so real to them, so down-to-earth. Today's children don't sit quietly with folded hands and absorb everything that's said to them. They question us. They say, "If it's really supposed to be like that, why isn't it?" And we've got to stop feeding them the old, pat answers that tell them very little about how it really is down here.

So one day I called the children to me, and we talked about family devotions. I could tell by their eyes, the expressions on their faces, that they were trying to resign themselves to the fact that Mother was going to reinstate family devotions and that was that. Ho hum! Instead I told them that we were going to try to be little Christs in the world, to try our best to do the things our Lord wants us to do.

"How are we going to know what He wants us to do?" Heide asked.

"Stupid! It's all in the Bible!" was Coke's brotherly reply.

"Yes," I said, "we'll have to rely on our Bibles a lot to be sure of what He expects of us."

"What are we going to *do* exactly?" Marie asked.

"Well," I explained, "for a long time we've been talking about a lot of things connected with our faith. We've talked about them at home, in Sunday school, in church. Now we're going to try and do them, not just talk about them. I mean really concentrate on it. In all phases of our lives we'll try our best to do as Jesus said we should."

"You mean like hearing about brotherly love" Marie said, "but never showing much of it?"

"Yep! And lots more. We'll have to take it a step at a time though, because I'm not real sure exactly where this is going to take us."

And we have changed since that day when

devotions became a drag and we decided to put our faith into action. We still pray together at mealtimes. We pray at night, each in his or her own room, alone, for that important person-to-person contact with God. There have been times when we've drawn together, arms around each other, tears close to the surface, and begged God for help and comfort. There have been other times when the drawing together has come out of shared happiness and the tears have been tears of joy and we've said together, "Thank You, God! Oh, thank You!" Prayer is very important to us, and it's growing increasingly more important. Not one of us is "afraid" or embarrassed to say, "Hey, will you all pray for me? I've got this problem and I need help."

We still go to Sunday school and church. It's all the same except we've added a new dimension to our lives, and this has made our faith vital and alive and a real part of the now scene. The children like it better, and so do I. And that's what this book is about—telling of the stumbling, groping ways in which we tried to exercise our faith: to be little Christs in the world. Don't think this is easy. There were times when we became discouraged almost to the point of giving up, but we're thankful there were also times of great satisfaction when we knew we were getting a little closer to the truths that Jesus talked about.

I HAD STARTED something, and now I had to come up with a plan of action. How do you go about being a little Christ in the world? How do you manage to wrest yourself from the safe security of your church and strike out on your own?

I thought deeply about this. I give the "expected" amount to the United Fund through a payroll deduction plan at work; I always buy at least two boxes of Girl Scout cookies; I give a tithe of my income (that's 10% before taxes) to the church. I willingly give to any emergency fund the pastor calls to our attention. But I realized that none of it was personal. In no case did I give myself along with the gift. I tried to think of one act of giving, outside of my family, in which I truly gave myself to such an extent that the amount of the gift became secondary. I couldn't think of one!

I talked to the children. "How can we be little Christs?" I asked them. They thought

I was asking them a question the way I so often do, knowing the answer, asking only to see if they knew it too. In this case, though, they were mistaken, and it worked to my advantage because they struggled to come up with the "right" answer.

"The only way we can be little Christs," Coke offered, "is to tell others about the Savior."

"Yeah," Heide agreed, "Love everybody and tell about Jesus."

Marie frowned, thought a minute, then said, "We're to go into the world and preach the Gospel."

"Hey, you really know what you're talking about," I said, "and it sounds great. Really great."

They all beamed. Smart kids.

"And," I continued, "it all sounded just as great when I heard it for the first time in Sunday school many years ago."

Three heads popped up. "What do you mean?"

"Look, I wasn't asking you for all those old pat phrases that sound so good. I'm talking about us. You're always saying we should get down to the nitty gritty. So let's do it. What can the four of us, Mom, Marie, Coke, and Heide, do to be little Christs in the world?"

There was a thinking silence for a little while, and finally Coke said, "I think I see

17

what you mean. To tell you the truth, I'll never go around telling kids about Jesus."

"Why not?"

"Are you kidding? They'd laugh at me, call me a nut."

"That's right, Mom," Heide said. "I told a whole bunch of kids in school that they're supposed to love everybody in the whole world because God said so, and they called me a dumb bunny."

"That really is the truth, Mom," Marie said. "If you try to talk about Jesus at school, the kids steer clear of you. They figure you're some kind of religious nut or something."

"Okay, I believe you. I know you're right. So what do we do?"

Marie shrugged. "Keep our faith to ourselves. What else?"

"Do you really think that's the answer, Marie?"

"Well, I know there are some religions where they go out and try to convert people and stuff like that, but after all, Lutherans just don't go for that kind of stuff."

"Well, then, God help us!" was all I could say.

"Well, Mom, do they?"

"I hope so, Marie. I sure hope so."

"But still, it isn't going to work if we go around slapping people on the back and saying, 'Jesus saves,' or asking them if they've been saved and stuff like that."

"There's got to be something else," I said. "Our Lord said we're to spread the Word."

Marie spoke, feeling her way. "Well, I suppose we just show people somehow how much Jesus means to us, and they'll see it, and then they'll want to have what we have."

"Like heck they will!" Heide snorted. "All the kids in my class know I love Jesus, because I tell them I love Him even more than I love my mother or my teacher, and they still call me a dumb bunny."

I got up. "I guess we'll think about this a little longer. And all of you pray that God will open a way for us, show us what to do."

I felt a little ridiculous and a little sad about a family who wanted to be little Christs in the world and didn't know how.

The next Sunday we came home from Sunday school and church and were walking from our car to our apartment. We were dressed in our Sunday best, and Heide was very proud of her new cape and hat and white gloves. We walked past a group of children dressed in blue jeans and play clothes. One of the little girls detached herself from the group and walked over to Heide. "Where have you been, Heide?" she asked.

Heide looked at the girl's slacks, then tugged daintily at her white gloves and answered, "We always go to Sunday school and church on Sunday. Always!" and she walked away, so help me, with her head in the air.

As soon as we entered the apartment, I gathered all three children around me.

"Heide," I said, "do you know what you just did?"

She shook her head.

"She acted like a little stuck-up brat," Coke said.

"No, she acted proud," Marie said. "So proud that she was all dressed up and had gone to Sunday school and church. She actually looked down her nose at that little girl."

Tears brimmed in Heide's eyes. "But she doesn't love Jesus, and I do!" she protested.

We ganged up on her then with love and explanations. Then we stood together, our bodies close, holding Heide in the circle of our love, and we prayed that God would take this pride away from our Heide and dump it somewhere.

"Well," Coke summed it up. "Maybe we don't know how to be little Christs in the world, but we sure know of one way not to be!"

I wasn't too encouraged so far. I had had more of a project in mind. One night we all sat down together and made a list of the things we could do to show our love, to be little Christs. Some things we had to eliminate. Like "preach the Gospel." We agreed that this was one way to share love, but we weren't preachers. We had to be practical and list the things we could do.

Our first list looked like this:

> Visit the sick (if anyone we know ever gets sick).
> Pray for others.
> Be a peacemaker.
> Don't sass people.
> Don't be proud and haughty about being a Christian.

That was it. So small! Was that all we could think of? I hoped we'd be able to add to this pitifully small list. More than that, that we'd soon find so many ways to be little Christs that we wouldn't see any need to make a list.

The next day Coke came home with the beautiful beginnings of a black eye.

"How did it happen?" I asked.

"This kid and I got into an argument. He put his foot right in my face."

"What did you do to him?"

"I didn't do anything. Christians don't fight."

"Well, you tried to make him stop, didn't you?"

Coke shook his head. "No, I just got away from him, that's all." Then he added, carefully touching his swollen eye, "Man, it's hard to be a Christian kid!"

When Heide heard about this, she was filled with righteous anger. "You should do what I always do, Coke," she said.

"What do you always do?"

"I tell them to stop because God said they are not to do that and they'd better stop, and I scream it at them real loud, too."

So Coke is trying to be a Christian kid, and he has a black eye. Heide is screaming and yelling about God and backing up her statements as if she were a personal messenger from God Himself.

Is this being little Christs in the world? I wondered.

Later Marie said, "Well, in a way, Heide's right. She pitches right in there and says, 'God said you're not to do that, so stop it.'"

"Just so she's sure she's right and God did say we're not to do whatever it is."

"And not be proud and haughty about it," Heide added with a grin.

"But Coke's right in his way too," Marie went on, "except for one thing."

"What's that?"

"When he stepped aside and refused to fight, he should have told the other boy why."

Coke laughed. "You mean tell him it was because I love Jesus? Man, I'd just have two black eyes then."

Marie's eyes were thoughtful pools of blue. "Maybe not, Coke," she said, "maybe not."

We finally decided that we were trying to be little Christs and that was all we'd said we'd do from the start. Just try, that's all.

ONE NIGHT WE were watching TV, and an appeal was made for starving children of the world.

Heide said, "I just can't stand it that there are starving children in this world."

Coke shook his head. "Me either. I don't like to think about it."

"There are ads in newspapers and magazines," I said, "where you can pledge to send twelve dollars a month to help buy food for at least one child. They send you the child's picture, and you can even send birthday and Christmas gifts to that child."

"Can you afford twelve dollars a month, Mom?" Heide asked.

"Me? You mean us, don't you? I certainly won't take away from my pledge to the church. And besides, we're all four of us trying to be little Christs."

"We don't have any money!"

"Yeah, you're the boss of the money in this family."

"Each one of you gets an allowance," I said. "You have candy and ice cream cones, you go to movies—"

"You mean we should give all that up?" Marie asked.

"Look," I answered, "it can't be called giving unless it's sacrificial. If we just skim some off the top of what we have, it's not giving."

"Sure it's giving," Marie protested. "If we skim twelve dollars off the top of what we have and send it to a starving child, that child is going to eat and live and not die of starvation."

Marie is 17 and loves to argue.

I got my Bible. "But we're talking about more than just giving so that someone doesn't starve. We've been doing that kind of giving all our lives. We want to give so that we give ourselves with the gift. If we give off the top, we haven't given anything of ourselves. It's not personal. But if we give up something we really want or enjoy, in order to give to someone who needs it, then we really give something of ourselves."

I opened my Bible. "In the sixth chapter of Galatians it says that we are supposed to carry the load for one another, that this is the way we obey the law of Christ. This means that if we have food and others are starving, we deny ourselves and give to them. They have a heavier load than we do, and it's up to us to help them carry it. In love."

"In other words, we really just have to love everybody."

"That's what it boils down to. Because, after all, we usually feel that our load in life is enough without having to carry anyone else's. It's only love that could make us want to help the other guy carry his too."

Marie nodded. "I see what you mean. If we give up something we want, so we can give to someone else, then that shows we really care about that person. That we care enough to give up something so they can—"

"What's wrong?" I asked. Marie had stopped in the middle of a sentence and the expression on her face was strange.

"When you think of it like that," she replied, "it sounds terrible."

"What do you mean?"

"Well, to say I'll give up candy and ice cream so some little child won't starve to death. Man, that sounds terrible!"

"Yes, it does sound terrible," Coke said. "What's ice cream and candy?"

"Maybe we have to dig a little deeper," I suggested.

Marie nodded. "I definitely think so."

"Okay. We need twelve dollars a month. How are we going to get it?"

"I'll give up candy," Heide said.

Marie sighed, but I ignored her.

"How much candy do you eat each week, Heide?" I asked.

"I always buy five cents worth at lunchtime at school," she answered.

"Every day?"

"Yes."

"So that's twenty-five cents a week from Heide."

Marie had pencil and paper in her hands now. "That's a dollar a month." she said. "We've got eleven dollars to go."

"I'll give twenty-five cents a week from my allowance," Coke said.

Marie was scribbling. "Two dollars a month. That's ten dollars to go."

"Let's give up dessert once a week," I said. "That would be at least one dollar a week."

Everyone agreed, and Marie said, "That makes six dollars and six to go."

All eyes turned to Marie. She looked at us and then grinned. "I'm thinking, I'm thinking!" she laughed.

"You could give up one ton a week of makeup," Coke said.

"Mind your own business, Coke!"

Heide giggled. "Marie could give up a gallon of perfume."

28

Marie said, "Maybe you two are trying to be little Christs in the world, but you're not doing too hot here at home!"

"Wait!" I interrupted. "Give Marie a chance to think of something."

"I've got it," Marie announced. "I'll give one dollar a week out of my allowance. That's four dollars a month, which means I'll have less money to save toward new clothes."

We all agreed that that would be sacrificial.

"Okay then," Marie said, "we now have ten dollars, and we still need two dollars."

"What are you giving up, Mom?" Heide asked.

"Me?"

"I was thinking that you could stop going to the beauty parlor."

"Yeah, Mom," Marie said, "You could wash your own hair."

"You have to be sacrificial the same as we do, don't you?"

So I gave up the luxury of going to the beauty parlor once a week, and we had $12 earmarked to help feed a starving child somewhere.

I was inclined to just withhold the money from their allowances and send a check each month to whichever children's fund we decided on. It was the easiest, most practical way to do it. But Coke changed my mind. He

got a cigar box from the grocery store, painted a cross on the cover, and handed it to me. "Here's our little Christ box," he said. "Every week we'll put in what we said we would."

"And every Friday night," Heide added, "instead of going to the beauty parlor, you put your money in the box."

Later Marie said, "That's a good idea. On the one day a week when we don't have dessert, we'll put the dollar in the box."

So I saw that they wanted to feel, by doing something, that they were really giving a part of themselves with each penny that went toward feeding a child.

Sometimes, as time went on, we'd find ourselves without the exact change needed, so we'd put in a slip of paper: "I. O. U. 25¢ — Heide." And there were a few times when one of the children would put his money in the box and say, "I've been praying for our child," or, "I'm so glad we can do this." Always the money was put in the box with a certain aura of ceremony, even if only for a moment. Coke would race up to the box on allowance day, his always grimy fingers clutching a quarter, his body already half turned to run in the other direction toward friends and play, but he'd stop, poised in flight, and open the box, put his money in, sometimes very quietly, sometimes grinning and saying, "Man, that's one thing I'll never forget."

Then, once a month, when we were all together, one of the children would count all the money and give it to me. Then I'd write out a check for $12 and address an envelope, and we'd mail a small part of ourselves to help one very small person somewhere in our world.

SO FAR SO GOOD, but I felt we needed to do more. We needed some person-to-person contact. I didn't know what, who, or how, but I decided to talk it over with the children and see what we could come up with.

"I feel that there must be more we can do," I said to them one evening. "I feel we should get out and have some person-to-person contact."

"Just what are you driving at, Mom?" Marie asked.

"Well, it's like making loincloths for natives—" I began.

"Loincloths? What's that got to do with what we're talking about?"

"I mean, like women sit in the church basement and sew loincloths for the dark-skinned natives of somewhere, and they feel good about it, like they've done their Christian duty toward their less fortunate brothers, but they've had no contact with anyone."

"Are loincloths things that are really needed?" Marie asked.

"I guess so. Women have been making them for as far back as I can remember."

The children started to giggle.

"Look, I'm not putting down the making of loincloths. I just mean, figuratively speaking, that I don't want to go on forever making loincloths."

They stopped giggling, but they were still waiting for an explanation.

"Let me put it another way," I went on. "Before any of you were born, I worked in a Lutheran children's home as a housemother. Once a year the children's home would put out a call for good, used clothing for the children in the home. They sent this plea to all the Lutheran churches in the area, and pretty soon the boxes of clothing would start coming in from the churches. They put all of the boxes upstairs in an attic room. One day the head housemother told me I could go up to the attic room and open some of the boxes and get some needed clothes for my group of eight- and nine-year-old girls. I went up there alone and started opening boxes, sorting through all the clothes to find suitable things for my girls. Some of the clothes were very nice—washed and ironed—and a few were brand new. But then I found clothing that was torn and ragged and dirty. I even found some underwear that was so dirty it stunk."

"What did you do?"

"Oh, I threw the junk away, but I felt so bad, I cried a little. On the boxes were labels that said, 'From the ladies of such and such Lutheran church,' or, 'Given by the congregation of such and such Lutheran church,' and I was ashamed. Those people, whoever they were, hadn't given one thought to the unfortunate children who were receiving this gift. Or worse, they'd said, 'This is good enough for them.' It just made me feel so sad to think that anyone could give a gift and give nothing of themselves along with it."

"That's terrible," Marie said, "just terrible. And I see what you mean, Mom, about some person-to-person contact."

"So do I," Coke agreed, "but where do we go? Who needs us?"

We thought about it for a few days without coming up with any answers. Then one day we passed a nursing home, near to where we lived, and the thought struck all of us. Old people in nursing homes would welcome company!

"They get lonely."

"They feel that nobody loves them anymore."

"We could sort of adopt a grandma."

I knew it was true. Old people are suddenly shifted from a position in society to a nonpersonal environment. They're confused, lonely, and perhaps a little resentful. They are in need of love. They are receiving everything else needful: care, food, a place to live, etc. They need only love.

"Yep," I agreed with the children. "We've got love filled up and brimming over. Let's share it!"

The next day we went to the nursing home. As we walked up the front steps, we talked about how nice it was going to be to have an adopted grandma. Child's talk. Simple child's talk, and I was swimming right along with them.

We knocked on the door, and a white-uniformed lady looked out at us through a closed screen door.

"Yes?"

I felt a little foolish. How did I start this ball rolling?

"I was a pastor's wife," I began, "and I used to go with him sometimes when he called on—" Oh! This was going so badly!

The white uniform stood stiffly behind the screen door, waiting.

"Well, you see, the children and I—"

Heide interrupted. "We want to adopt one of your grandmas," she said.

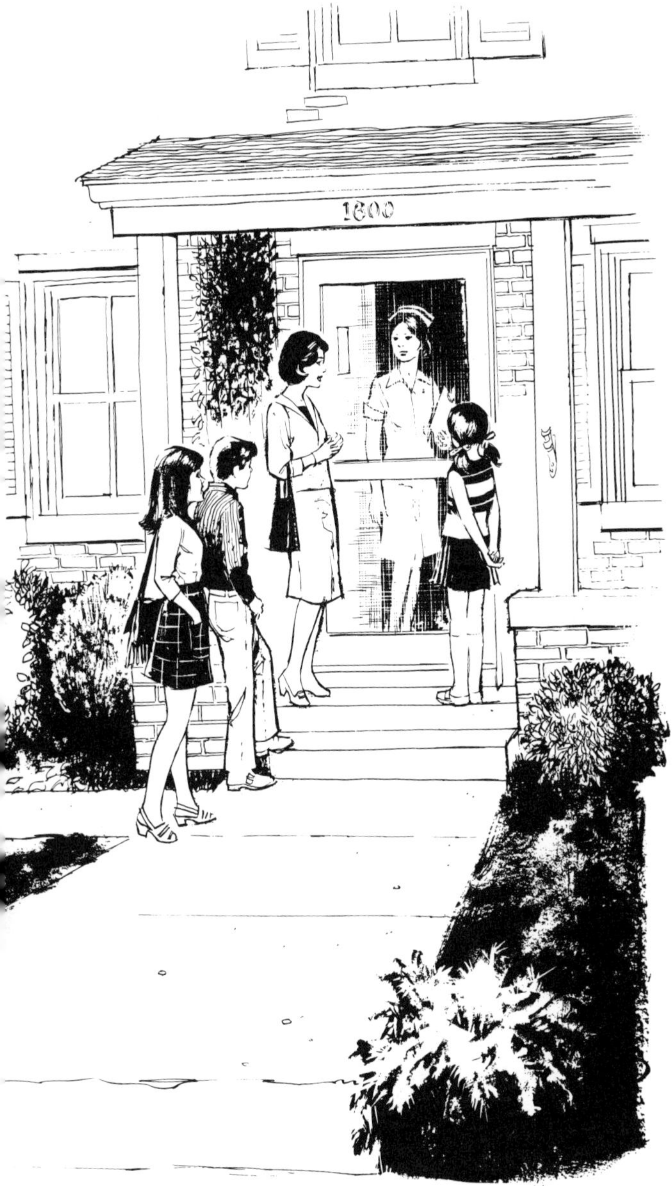
1800

So there it was. And then I was able to explain to the woman exactly what we had in mind. That we didn't want to appear as Lady Bountiful and her fat children bearing alms, but that we had love and companionship to give and we very much wanted to give it. Was it needed? Or welcome?

No, it wasn't. The woman said, "All of our patients either have families that visit them regularly, or else the patients are senile and visitors would disturb them."

"That surprises me," I said. "I remember so well when I went with my husband to nursing homes. There were always several women who sat alone in their rooms, who never had visitors, and they were so lonely."

The woman shook her head. "Not here."

"We don't represent any organization," I went on, "We are exactly what we seem to be. Just a family—"

She nodded. "I understand."

"We just want to ease the loneliness of someone."

She shook her head again. "There aren't any like that here."

We turned and started for the car. I didn't want to talk to her anymore.

"Maybe you could try a convalescent home," she called after us.

I said thanks over my shoulder as we hurried to the car.

"Don't worry," I said to the children. "Someplace in this town is someone who will be glad to have our friendship."

The following Sunday I asked our pastor if he knew someone who would welcome our visits and our friendship. "You see," I explained, "we want very much to practice our faith. To try to be little Christs."

He looked astonished at my request. He couldn't seem to think of an answer.

Finally he said, "I'll let you know. Soon."

I've known of churches in large cities where the congregation has a special fund and perhaps used clothing and canned goods on hand. Should a person come to that church or the parsonage during the week, the pastor has an emergency closet, or whatever it's called, that he can go to for whatever is needed. He gives from this closet at his own discretion and is never questioned about how he's used its contents. (Why doesn't anyone ever ask? Aren't they interested beyond bringing a can of something now and then or putting a few dollars into the fund?)

Sometimes, especially when it's a particularly "interesting case," the pastor will tell the people how some of the contents of their emergency fund were put to use. But usually there is no more personal contact than there is for the natives who receive the loincloths.

In our churches we have committees for everything. Even special committees to keep track of the silverware in the kitchen and to keep a count of the church-owned tablecloths. But I don't know of a church that has a committee whose sole job is to keep the members informed of the needy in the community—regardless of church affiliation. If I ever hear of a committee like that, I'll beg to serve on it. This committee would find out what was needed in the community. Is there an elderly person living alone? Could she use some help with driving, shopping, etc.? Maybe she'd welcome visitors now and then to ease the loneliness. Is there a widow with a little boy who worries because that little boy is growing up with no male influence in his life? Is there some father in the congregation who would be willing to share a few fishing hours with this boy?

This would involve a lot of groundwork for the committee—a lot of personal contact. A lot of work? Yes! And there would be doors slammed in well-meaning faces, and good people would be taken advantage of, but *what is the church all about?* We aren't supposed to huddle together and warm ourselves by the light of our faith. That fire is to burn brighter than any other, and we're to step back and widen our circle to include the world.

ONE DAY COKE SAID, "Mom, I wonder why it is that nobody wants us to visit them."

Before I could answer, Heide said, "If nobody wants us, we won't go and that's that!"

"But we don't know that nobody wants us," I said, "we just haven't found anyone yet."

That night I wrote a letter to a church-owned old people's home. I said nothing to the children about it. If I received an answer, telling us we were welcome, it would be time enough to tell them. Perhaps it was my motherly protective instinct working overtime, but I didn't want to walk them up to another door and have it closed in our faces. Not yet. I guess I was afraid they'd want to quit before we'd really started.

In the meantime we were praying that if there were some way—some place—where we could be used, God would open the way to us.

"It's pretty obvious," Marie remarked, "that nobody but God is going to open any ways for us."

Coke asked, "Even when we do find things to do—I mean, being little Christs—we're still going to go to church and Sunday school, aren't we?"

"Of course we are. We need very much to go to church and Sunday school to hear God's Word and learn more about His will for our lives and also for the fellowship with other Christians."

"You mean like at the potluck dinners?"

"Yes, but also when we worship together and receive the Lord's Supper together and sing hymns together."

Coke nodded. "So we'll still be going to the potluck dinners?"

"Yep!"

"Good! I was afraid they were out."

Poor Coke! He doesn't mind in the least bit being sacrificial when it comes to time, money, and love, but when you touch on the subject of food, you're treading on dangerous ground!

We've talked about this a lot, my children and I. We're out to be little Christs in the world to the best of our ability. We're willing to work very hard at it because it's an expression of our faith, and we believe this is what Christianity is all about. We'll keep on going to our church to hear God's Word and to get the needed strength to then go out into His world and try to be like He was—like He said we should be. I didn't say, and the children didn't ask, "What if we don't get those things at church? Do we still go?"

Yes, we'll keep on going, serving where we can, learning, and thanking God for the church. But I have given it a lot of thought, and there are things in my heart.

Dear pastor: You know, I really don't care much what you do. Wear a turned-around collar or don't; kneel, stand, whatever pleases you. Have guitar players strolling the aisles, trumpets and flutes, whatever you want to try, it's all right with me. I will never criticize you for trying to generate some life and interest in your congregation. But, dear pastor, when you walk up to that pulpit, please think of me. There may be some who come to church, and all they're thinking of is the roast in the oven or Mrs. Jones's new hat, but I'm here too, and there are others like me.

I sit down in my pew every Sunday and my mind and body are expectant, for now I will hear God. He will talk to me and comfort and strengthen and instruct me. I need it so much and I sit there, my eyes turned toward the pulpit—waiting. Talk about being turned on! Every Sunday I'm turned on and tuned in.

So please, pastor, bring God's Word to me, and don't tiptoe around the edges of it so as to spare my feelings. I want Law and Gospel— rightfully divided—and I need it. Maybe you

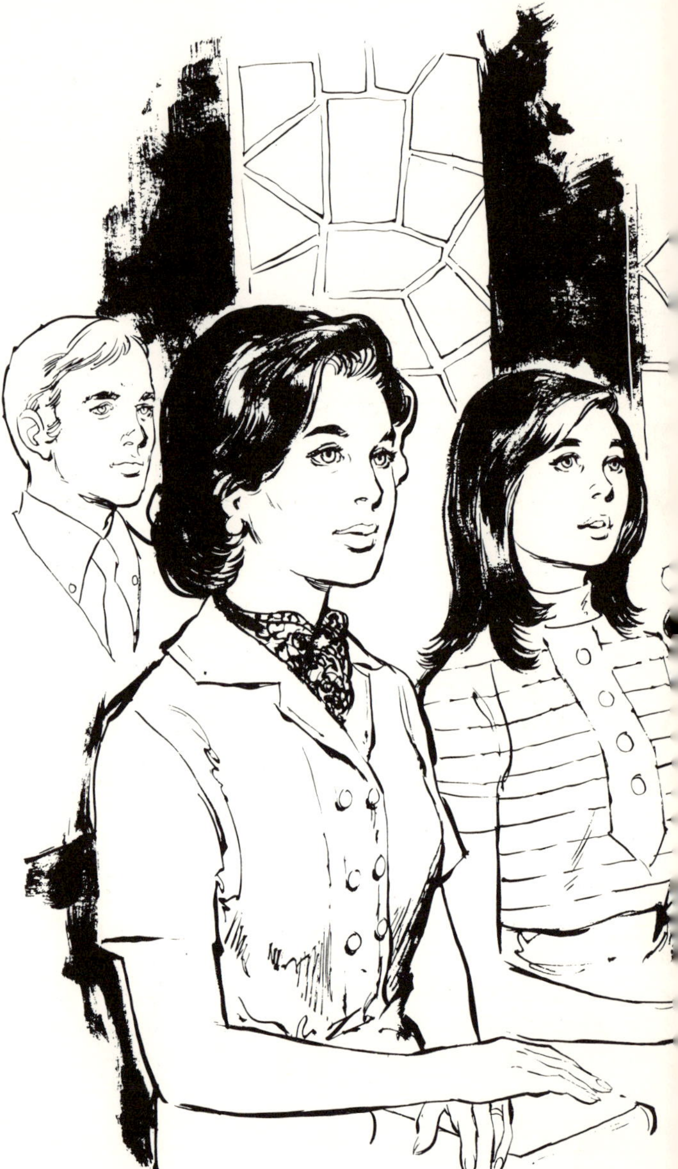

won't use perfect English or big, theological-sounding words. You may falter now and then or lose your place or mispronounce a word—

believe me, I'll hardly notice and never remember. It won't matter at all. The only thing that matters is that I came to church and I heard God talking to me.

And dear Sunday school teacher: Please plan and prepare your lessons with great care and much prayer. Please pray for wisdom so that you will be able to look into my child's eyes on Sunday morning and impart a real, living spark of faith to him. Please take your job seriously, and make him know that Jesus Christ is everything to you and that you couldn't make it one day without Him. (And if this isn't true, may your teaching days be short-lived. If possible, I'll help see to it.)

Please don't spend that precious hour doing nothing but making cute little cutouts, even if they are cutouts of Jesus. And don't bore him to tears. In my opinion it's as much a sin to bore our people to death with the Gospel as it is to waste their time. If you're truly on fire with the message of Jesus Christ and you want desperately to put that fire in the heart of a child, don't worry! You won't bore him.

As I see it, worship in church has a very real purpose, and that is to help us deepen our response to all of God's people. In the perfect light of Christ's love I can correct my own love. Through our worship experiences we find the power to become a truly reconciled community. To honestly know and believe that all men are brothers.

One day the children and I were talking about this, and I opened my Bible to John 21:15-18.

"Our Lord was talking to Peter," I began, "and He looked at him and said, 'Peter, do you love Me?'"

"I'll bet Peter said yes."

"He not only said yes, but I guess he was a little surprised at the question, because he answered, 'Lord, You *know* I do!'"

"Then what did Jesus say?"

"He told Peter to feed His lambs, and then He just kept looking at Peter, and soon He asked him again, 'Peter, do you love Me?'"

"Oh, brother! What did Peter say this time?"

"He said again, 'Lord, You *know* I do!'"

"I would have said, 'Why do You keep asking me?'"

"Well, Jesus just asked him a third time, 'Peter, do you love Me?'"

"I guess that's one way to make you really think hard about the question."

"And," I continued, "for the third time Peter answered, 'Lord, You *know* I do.' Probably his answer had more of what we call the ring of truth to it that third time."

"I can't figure out why Jesus kept asking him like that," Coke said.

"Me either," Heide added.

"Well, what Jesus said next answers that question. He said, 'Then feed My sheep.' In other words, 'If you love Me as you say you do, you'll feed My sheep.'" I waited, then asked, "Who are Christ's sheep?"

"All the people in the world," Heide answered.

"Yeah," Coke said, "He's the Shepherd and we're the sheep."

"So how are we to feed His sheep?"

"Give food?"

"And money to buy food?"

"Well, I think of other things. Lonely people need to be fed with friendship, and troubled people need to be fed with help. Things like that."

"What it boils down to," Marie said, "is just trying to find out what other people need and then giving it to them if you can."

"So," I summed it up, "we come back to our worship. Christ is asking us, 'Do you love Me?' and in our worship we're answering Him, 'Lord, You *know* we do!' and He is saying, 'Then feed My sheep.' And so we know that going to church is necessary, but it isn't enough. We only get to the point of a question and an answer—a command. We have to leave the church each Sunday and go out into His world and feed His sheep. With love and concern."

LITTLE BY LITTLE, in His own good and wise time, God showed us ways in which we could be little Christs. Ways in which we could show our love.

It was near the Christmas season, and one day I saw a little article in the newspaper about a crippled boy who was confined to his home and would welcome visitors. I read the article to the children, and they were enthusiastic about visiting this boy, whose name, the newspaper said, was Jimmy.

On a cold, wet, gloomy day we decided to go to Jimmy's house. We decided that, although we knew it wasn't necessary, we'd like to take a small gift to Jimmy. And of course, even this small gift had to be sacrificial. Each of us dug down in our pockets and we came up with enough to buy a small Christmas decoration for Jimmy.

Coke kept the city map and a pencil on his knee and told me which streets to look out for, when to turn, and before too long we pulled up in front of a little frame building with a big sign: JIMMY'S PLACE.

As we were getting out of the car, a small woman walked out to us. "I know you're Mrs. Mall and Marie and Coke and Heide," she said. "We've been waiting for you." I had written beforehand telling them we would like to visit Jimmy, and this welcome from Jimmy's mother was wonderful.

She led us into the store. Their whole store and the rooms they lived in were about as big as the average suburban living room and family room. It was very crowded, but Jimmy's mother quickly brought chairs, and we sat in a little circle, our knees nearly touching. Jimmy sat in his wheelchair. We knew from the newspaper item that he was almost completely paralyzed from the neck down, we knew that he was not a "boy" but 28 years old, and so his crippled, twisted body was what we expected. His grey hair was no surprise either. However, what we weren't prepared for was that Jimmy couldn't talk. His tongue also was paralyzed. When he wanted to say something, he muttered a series of grunts, and his mother would listen to him, nod her head, and then interpret. It was amazing until I realized that she probably knew what he was thinking, what sort of a response he would make, and so in that way she interpreted.

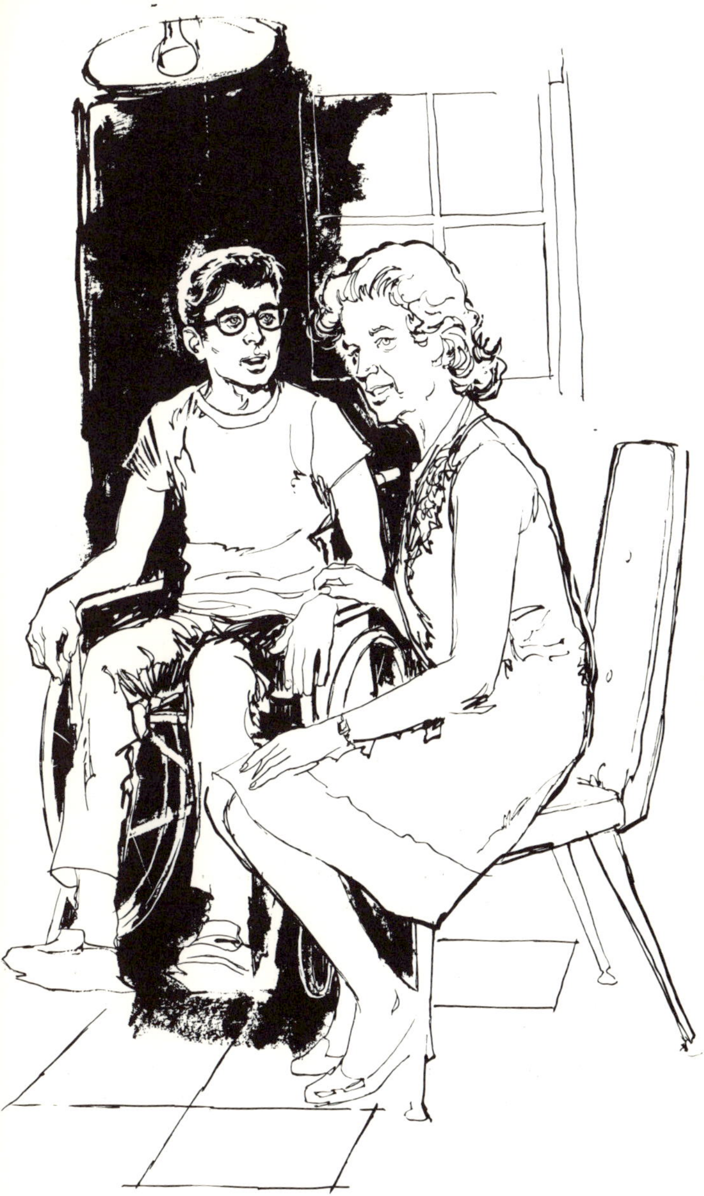

Coke tried to talk to Jimmy about fishing. And Jimmy pointed to the many pictures of fish he had on the wall. He also had pictures of dogs and horses.

Heide, usually the one who embarrasses us by loving and hugging and kissing anyone she meets, was absolutely tongue-tied. She sat next to Jimmy, her little back stiff and straight, her feet placed side by side in front of her, her hands folded in her lap, and looked at Jimmy mostly out of the corner of her eye.

Jimmy's mother brought the children a bottle of pop, and then she showed us a picture of Jimmy when he was 5 years old. I looked at the picture of a beautiful little boy. When I looked closer, I could see that one leg was shorter than the other and that his hands had a slightly twisted appearance. But I had to look very closely. She told us how, just at the time when Jimmy was 5, his father had died, and she was left with her son, growing progressively more crippled and twisted.

"I decided right from the beginning," she said, "that Jimmy was going to have as full a life as possible." At first he was ashamed of his body and always wanted to keep it covered so that no one could see it, and he never wanted to eat in front of others because he couldn't manage it very well. "But," she continued, "I didn't let him start that. 'Don't be ashamed of what you are,' I told him. And to this day he isn't ashamed."

Then Jimmy started to "talk," and I was amazed to discover that I could figure out pretty much what he was saying. He told us that he was so thankful for his eyes, that he could see people and pictures and for his hearing, that he could hear people talk. "And," he continued, "someday—a day I wait for— I will be with Jesus, and I won't be like this anymore."

We talked for well over an hour and then got up to leave. I looked at Jimmy, a twisted heap piled into a wheelchair, and impulsively I put a hand on his cheek and held it there, and said, "Good-bye, Jimmy. We'll be back. God love you."

Jimmy didn't try to talk, but his eyes said so much!

On the way out to the car I asked his mother if there was anything she needed, any help, and she said no. "Just come and see him again," she said.

The drive back home was a very quiet one. Every once in a while one of us would break the silence:

"Just think! All he could say was that he was thankful that he can see."

"And hear."

"And knowing that someday he'll be straight and whole when he's with Jesus."

"Just think of it!"

We took very little to Jimmy. The inexpensive Christmas decoration and ourselves. We came away with so much! For days and days we were filled with thanksgiving to a God who had been so good to us, who had given Jimmy such a measure of faith and had given his dear mother so much love and strength. We couldn't stop talking about it.

Since then there have been many visits to Jimmy. We laugh and talk together. Sometimes we bring a gift, most often not. Once in a while we bring a special picture that Heide has drawn for Jimmy. Heide no longer sits stiffly apart from Jimmy, and they're great friends. Once, when she rose to leave and started to put on her coat, Jimmy's clawlike hands reached out to her. They grasped at her shoulders and fumbled on her back. Heide turned and smiled and said, "I love you, Jimmy." Later, on the way home, she said, "Did you see how Jimmy was trying to be a gentleman? He was trying to help me with my coat!"

So we visit Jimmy, and we love him, but we always get more than we can possibly give. And that was the first time, but certainly not the last, that we discovered it's always that way when you give in Christ's name and because of Him and His love. You get back more than you can ever give.

THE ADJUSTMENT to an old people's home is a traumatic experience for individuals who have raised families, been father and breadwinner, mother and wife. They've raised their children, cooked, worked — all the things we're doing now. And then they're old and helpless, and they're often alone and afraid and maybe resentful.

After running a home or being in the business world, running their own lives, they are like children, having to obey certain rules, having to sit and wait for attention, having to live with others and get along with them.

They're homesick for what they once had but is now lost to them for as long as they live. They are usually grounded. This building, this room, perhaps this path through a garden — this is their world now, and they have to rely on their memories of what the outside world is like. Perhaps if they could go out, it would tire and confuse them — but to *never* see it and smell it again?

Their health isn't what it once was—they can't see quite as well or hear all they once could. Perhaps they're worried about money. "Will it hold out for as long as I must be here?" And the worst of all is the feeling of absolute uselessness. "Nobody needs me for anything!"

It is sad, and it sounds hopeless—but there is a solution. The Bible tells us that our "religion" is not enough. To go to church, to kneel and pray, to sing hymns can never be enough. To worship God means also to care about others. To care deeply about another's hunger, his loneliness, *him.*

We can do a lot for these old people. We can drop in from time to time on a regular basis. Run errands for them, take them on short drives or shopping trips; bring the children always—take them to visit old and dear friends who are ill or hospitalized. If we're looking for something relevant to do, here it is!

I had written to the old folk's home in our town, and I had received an answer. A very kind, welcoming letter but one that expressed a wonder about what to do with just one unorganized family. Sure, church groups came to the home on a regular basis: luncheons, parties, etc., were given. But just a family? No organization? Perhaps you'd like to join in with one of the groups who come here regularly.

I gave up. Forget it!

And then one Sunday when we got home from church and had eaten lunch, I plopped down on the couch, grateful for a few hours to read or think, to do what I wanted to do. I work hard all week, and my few free hours on Sundays are precious to me.

"Mom, did you ever write to that old folk's home?" Marie asked.

"Yes, I did."

"Did they answer you?"

"Well, yes, but it seems that people have to be organized nowadays. I mean, if you don't represent a group or an organization, they don't know how to accept you. Or what to do with you."

"Oh, phooey!"

"They were very nice, and they did welcome us—but, well, what could they say, really?"

Marie stood up. "Why don't we just go out there?"

"We will, Marie."

"No, I mean now. Just go out there and talk to some of the old people."

"I'm not sure—"

"Yeah," Coke interrupted, "why not?"

"We'll sure never find a grandma to adopt sitting here," Heide said.

So away we went. Coke grabbed the city map, and we drove to the old folk's home. The

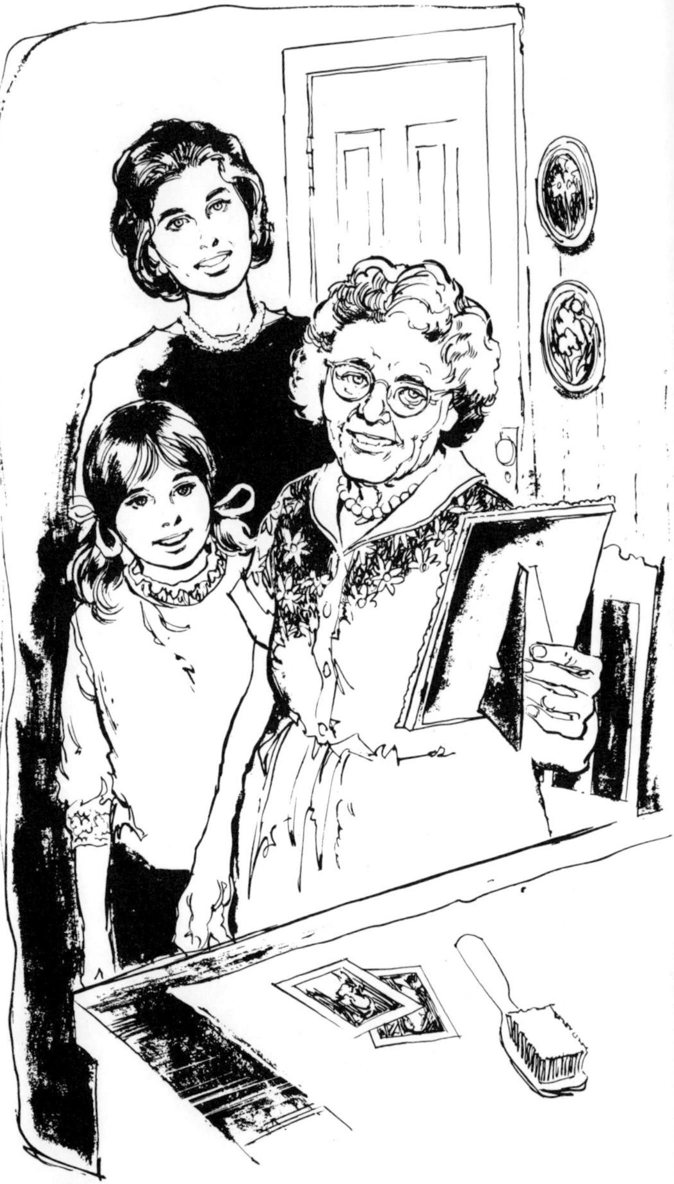

front door was unlocked, and we walked in. We walked down a few hallways, peeked into the dining room, out at the lovely garden. Then we saw a group of about 12 women sitting in a semicircle. They were all dressed in their Sunday best, and they were waiting. For visitors, we supposed.

We entered the room, shyly, hoping we weren't intruding, wondering about our welcome. Immediately 12 heads turned and started talking to us.

"Hello! Where are you from?"

"Come here, little girl. Tell me your name."

"What's your name, son?"

We were enveloped! Never have we ever felt so welcomed by anyone!

After a few minutes of conversation one of the women rose and said, "Let me show you around."

We followed her, and she showed us the chapel and several other rooms, and then she whispered, "I'm going to show you my room."

In her room we looked at pictures. "This was my sister when she was a young girl."

"These are my great-grandchildren."

"This is my wedding picture."

Within a few minutes we felt like family. Loneliness makes people reach out to others in a warm, welcome way.

OUR LIST, so meager at the beginning, has grown so long that we don't make lists anymore. After one year it's become a way of life for us, penetrating into every area and facet of our existence. We share as a family when we visit Jimmy or our dear little lady at the old folk's home, but we are also trying to be little Christs on a personal basis—not especially as a family each time. We share our experiences with each other, and we talk a different language too. Where once we rather looked down on "those" people who always said, "Dear brother (sister) in Christ," or who constantly talked about the Spirit moving them, now it's a part of our language too because we understand it now and it has meaning for us. It's not unusual now for one of the children to say, "A brother started spitting at me today. Know what I did? I asked for an extra share of the Spirit, and I just looked at him. And to myself I thought, 'I love you, my brother, I love you!' real hard, and pretty soon he stopped spitting, and later on we were friends."

These things didn't come to us all at once, but because of our attitudes and our thinking and our searching we've seen the opportunities. Surely they existed before, but we weren't aware of them. And now words like the Spirit and brother and sister have a very deep meaning to us.

I read this somewhere and I shared it with the children:

Did you ever see a Christian turn his cheek when slapped?
—I never did.
Take off his coat and give it to a bum on the street?
—I never did.
Feed his enemy?
—I never did.
Pray for some cuss who'd cheated him?
—I never did.

"This being little Christs means this too," I said. "Our everyday encounters with people."

We're very much aware of the ecological crisis, and we talk about the things we can do like using certain kinds of soap and not littering; but the biggest problem seems to be the population explosion. I can remember going shopping and not having to stand in a line, not bumping into someone at every

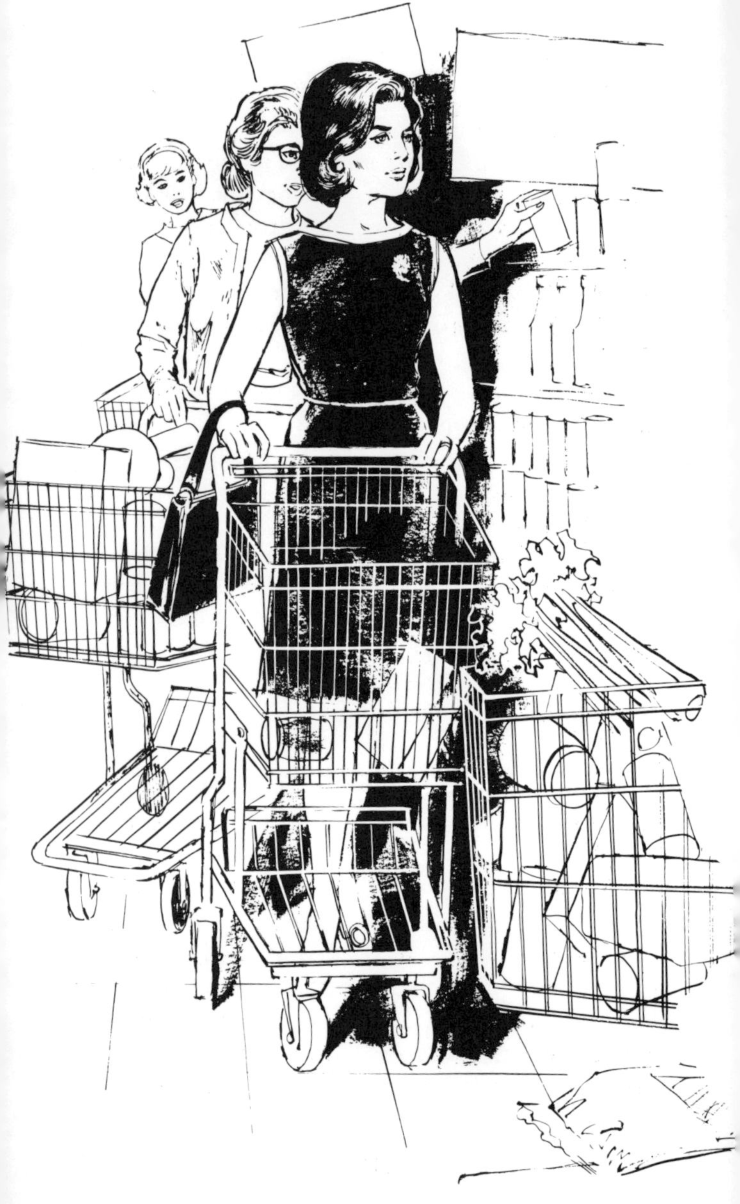

corner; I recall Sunday afternoon drives—for pleasure. I remember quiet, uncrowded paths and lonely stretches of beach. Today we stand in line for everything we do, and we shove and push and honk our way through the traffic of people.

One day we had all been shopping together. We drove through traffic to the shopping center, finally found a place to park. In the store we dodged women with shopping carts, managed to grab what we wanted off the shelves, pushed our way into a line at the check-out counter, and dragged our way back to the car. The ride home was silent, grim, and by the time we got home I was exhausted, nervous, and edgy. "People!" I exploded. "I've about had enough of people!"

"Hey, Mom," Coke said with a half-smile. "People are those things we're supposed to love so much, remember?"

That stopped me. Oh, he was so right! And I needed so much to be reminded.

Later, when I was calm, we discussed this. A very special problem had arisen. We were to love all people—to try to be little Christs in the world. Okay. And the Bible didn't say, "As long as there aren't too many people around."

I had read about an experiment on the stress factor of overpopulation. When some deer were put in a field, each with so much space for itself, everything was fine. But when they increased the number of deer within the same space, stress caused the deer to become nervous, ill, and in some cases to die for no apparent reason.

We talked about this and decided that, in order to try to be little Christs, we had to get along with our fellowman even if there are too many of us around. And so now, when we're out in the car and someone behind us starts honking, we all smile.

"There's some poor soul getting nervous," we say.

"Let's pray for him."

"Hey, brother back there in that car. We love you!"

Okay, maybe it doesn't do a thing for that man leaning on his horn, but it sure does something for us. Even when you give love silently, you get more than you give. And whenever it's possible, we also let him pass, let him have his way so that he won't get any more upset than he is.

When we're shopping, we move out of the other person's way. We let her pass if she seems to be in a hurry. And we do it with a smile and a gracious manner. In the line we look to see if the person behind us has fewer items than we do. If so, we ask her to go ahead of us. And when a woman, for example, shoves me or bangs into my shopping cart in order to get ahead of me, I step out of the way and smile, and I say to myself, "Dear sister, I love you. You don't know it, but I do."

You may say that it all boils down to just simple courtesy, and maybe it does, but our motive is love. We earnestly try to feel genuine love in our hearts for every man, woman, and child on the face of this earth. And because we have this love in our hearts, we honestly don't want to push anyone out of the way or try to beat him to a place in line or be rude to him.

Anyway, it's working for us, and as with all of God's way, we receive more than we can give. We're so much happier and at peace with His world. And I can't help wondering what it would be like if every one of us tried this.

A teen-ager came to me recently with a problem. She didn't come to me willingly; she was dragged, so to speak, by someone else. I imagine last year I would have made all the mistakes we older people always make with teen-agers. I would have been critical, talked too much, given too much advice, scolded. And the teen-ager would have gone away hating me, her problem unsolved.

But this time, as we sat down together, I thought, "I love this girl. I have nothing in my heart but love for her right at this moment, and I want to help her. God, help me to help her. I love her."

And as a result I sat next to her, and I listened to her talk. Little by little, as she realized that I was going to continue listening, that I was really interested in what she had to say, she talked more freely.

She went around and around the problem, telling *her* side of the story, how she wasn't understood by anyone, until finally, all by herself, she came full circle and began to admit where maybe she'd been at fault too and maybe there were a few things she could do — and sometime during that long monolog my hands had reached out and touched hers, and she had slipped a hand into mine, and we sat there touching each other, my love for her a very strong thing.

Later, after she'd talked herself into the beginning of a solution to her problem and I'd said very little, she rose to leave.

"Thanks," she said. "You really helped."

"I didn't do very much," I answered.

"Oh, yes, you did! I was expecting a sermon. But you really *listened* to me. That was the best kind of a sermon!"

When she'd gone, I thanked God for showing me the way. Without love in my heart I'd never have been able to do it.

I'M SURE THERE are some who would find this very difficult to understand. But it happened, and this same sort of thing is happening to me and my children all the time:

There is a man in a parking lot. He collects the money each day, and I had to come into contact with him every morning, five mornings a week. He was crabby, practically impossible to get along with. Nearly everyone I knew who parked there hated him. My natural inclination was to have as little as possible to do with him, put him in his place. Instead I said to myself, "Mr. Parking Lot Attendant, my brother, whatever your name is, I love you. I really love you, and I'm going to make you know it." And I prayed that his disposition would sweeten and that somehow he would know that I truly loved him as my brother. I told the children about it and asked them to pray too.

With that in my mind and heart every morning my patience knew no limits. He couldn't make me angry. It wasn't long before he softened, and now that man and I are friends. He greets me pleasantly every morning, "Hi there, my little lady! How are you?"

He gives me a good parking space. We're friends. I've told him about my children, and he's told me about his wife and his children. And nobody can tell me that this could have been accomplished without the ingredient of love.

There may be some who question the relevance of our Christian faith in this world, but we don't. Not any more. Faith and love, the things Jesus talked about, they're here and now, as relevant today as they were when they were first spoken.

One year ago we set out to try and prove how relevant and workable our faith is. To see for ourselves if it was all a pile of good-sounding words listened to on Sunday morning and not very practical outside the walls of the church. We know now that it is possible

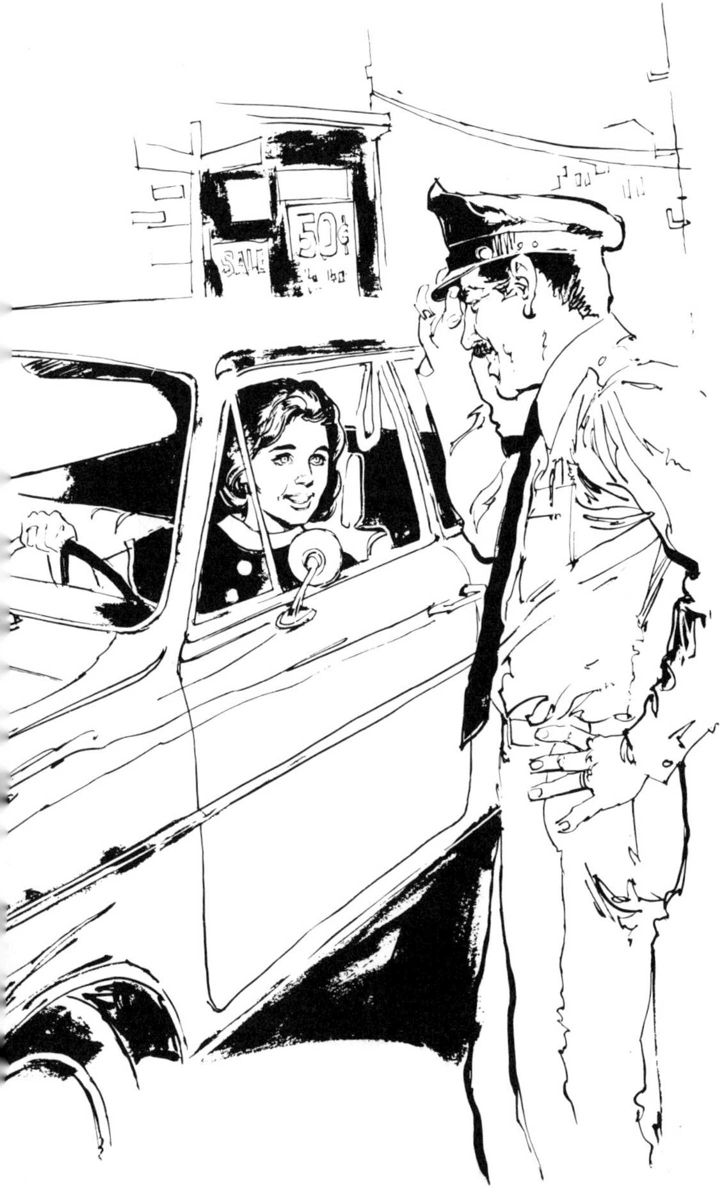
SALE
50¢

to be little Christs—oh, so very *little* ones! It is possible to follow His teachings in our everyday world—it works! We've touched a number of lives, but mostly they've made deep impressions on us. We're more tolerant of others because we have this love for everyone and it's helped us more than we've been able to help anyone. In every case we've tried to give of ourselves and our love and our money, and in every case we've received more than we've given. Our own problems are solved by helping others. To some—to one who hasn't tried it, it might sound silly. Imagine going around thinking to yourself, "Brother, I love you!" or, "Sister, down deep in my heart I really love you." Some might say, "Why, that's not Lutheran! That's more like holy-roller stuff!" (God forgive them.) But it's Lutheran all right. And Episcopalian and Baptist and Methodist and Roman Catholic—you name it—because it's Christian. It's what Jesus told us to do: Love all men. Feed My sheep. Love them. All the way. All men are my brothers in Christ, and I must love them all.

"Since you are God's dear children, you must try to be like Him. Your life must be controlled by love, just as Christ loved us and gave His life for us as a sweet-smelling offering and sacrifice which pleases God." Ephesians 5:1-2.

I WOULD VERY MUCH like to have a feedback from all the readers of this book. I hope and pray that many of you will decide to try what we tried, and I would like to hear from you. I want to hear about your failures, your disappointments, and your wonderful successes, like those we have experienced. A very big part of this has been the sharing of it within our family circle. Like when I came home the first time and told the children about the parking-lot attendant. They all promised to pray for him, and at the dinner table, when we join hands and pray, one of us each night would remember the parking-lot man and offer a special prayer. The night I came home from work and said to the children, "He smiled this morning!"

"He did!"

"Yep. And he said, 'How are you this morning, my little lady?'"

"'My little lady.' Oh, no!"

"Oh, yes! Isn't it great?"

We all shared something wonderful in that moment. And now I would like to share that circle of loving concern to include as many of our brothers and sisters as possible. Ask us to pray for you, for your own special projects—you know we will! Anyway, we'd like to hear from you.

One time in the car we were all saying, "Old lady back there, leaning on your horn, we love you!"

"Yes, sister of ours, we love you, and we wish you'd stop beating your brains out on that horn. Calm down!"

And Marie said, "You know what? We sound like fools."

"We sure do," I replied. "Fools for Christ."

So maybe we are. Fanatics about this love business. Fools for Christ. Join the club! And let us hear what you're doing.